A One-Act Comedy for Girls

by

ANNE COULTER MARTENS

PAJAMA PARTY

THE DRAMATIC PUBLISHING COMPANY

*** NOTICE ***

The amateur and stock acting rights to this work are controlled exclusively by THE DRAMATIC PUBLISHING COMPANY without whose permission in writing no performance of it may be given. Royalty fees are given in our current catalogue and are subject to change without notice. Royalty must be paid every time a play is performed whether or not it is presented for profit and whether or not admission is charged. A play is performed anytime it is acted before an audience. All inquiries concerning amateur and stock rights should be addressed to:

DRAMATIC PUBLISHING
P. O. Box 129., Woodstock, Illinois 60098

ISBN 0-87129-289-0

PAJAMA PARTY

A Comedy in One Act

FOR TEN GIRLS

CHARACTERS

GINNY . . . . *who gives the party*

MRS. REDMOND . . . . *her mother*

SANDY . . . . *her younger sister*

NAN . . . . *her best friend*

PHYLLIS
BECKY
CARLA
ELLIE } . . . . *guests*

MICKY . . . . *a stranger*

HELEN . . . . *a late-comer*

PLACE: *Ginny's and Sandy's bedroom.*

TIME: *The present. Evening.*

CHART OF STAGE POSITIONS

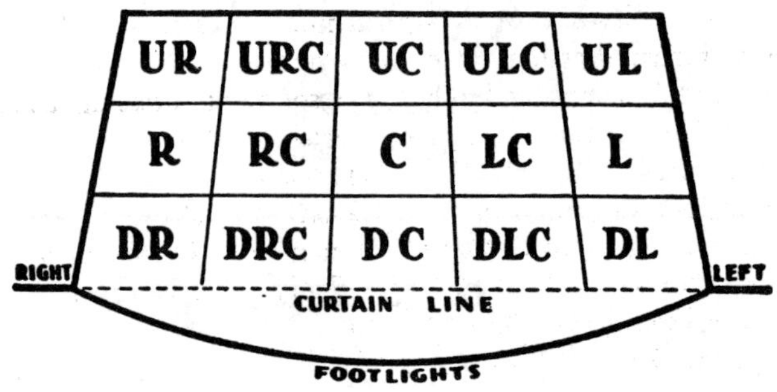

STAGE POSITIONS

Upstage means away from the footlights, *downstage* means toward the footlights, and *right* and *left* are used with reference to the actor as he faces the audience. R means *right,* L means *left,* U means *up,* D means *down,* C means *center,* and these abbreviations are used in combination, as: U R for *up right,* R C for *right center,* D L C for *down left center,* etc. One will note that a position designated on the stage refers to a general territory, rather than to a given point.

NOTE: Before starting rehearsals, chalk off your stage or rehearsal space as indicated above in the *Chart of Stage Positions.* Then teach your actors the meanings and positions of these fundamental terms of stage movement by having them walk from one position to another until they are familiar with them. The use of these abbreviated terms in directing the play saves time, speeds up rehearsals, and reduces the amount of explanation the director has to give to his actors.

PROPERTIES

GENERAL: Twin beds, with matching covers and gay lounging cushions; dressing table, with mirror on wall above it; two boudoir lamps and other accessories on dressing table; small bench; high-backed chair; magazine rack and floor lamp; table or desk, with telephone, telephone book and other small articles; record player and records on small stand; pennants, school souvenirs, etc.; magazines on both beds and on floor, and cushions scattered about on floor; umbrella on bed L; small box for club money on table D L.

CARLA: Overnight bag.
BECKY: Overnight bag.
MICKY: Flashlight.
PHYLLIS: Overnight bag.
ELLIE: Overnight bag.
GINNY: Dishes of candy and potato chips.
SANDY: Blue paper to cover flashlight.
HELEN: Music roll.

PRODUCTION NOTE

Nothing adds more to the polish of a production than the quick picking up of cues. Unless there is a definite reason for a pause, train your actors to come in with their speeches "on the heels," so to speak, of the preceding speeches. When a production lags, audience interest likewise will lag.

It is always advisable during the last week of rehearsals to hold one or more sessions during which the actors merely sit around in a circle and go through lines only with the express purpose of snapping up cues.

PAJAMA PARTY

SCENE: *The scene is the bedroom shared by Ginny and Sandy. Twin beds of the day bed type are against the* R *and* L *walls of the room. The beds have attractive matching covers and gay lounging cushions. Against the rear wall,* U C, *is a dressing table, with a mirror on the wall above it. On the dressing table, among the usual accessories, are two boudoir lamps. In front of the dressing table is a small bench. In the* U R *corner of the room is a chair with a rather high back. Left of this chair are a magazine rack and a floor lamp. A door* D L *leads to the front part of the house, while a door* U R *leads to some other rooms. Downstage of the* D L *door is a small table or desk, with a telephone, telephone book and other small articles. At* D R *stage is a small stand with a record player and some records. Pennants, school souvenirs and the usual articles found in a young girl's room complete the setting.*]

AT RISE OF CURTAIN: *The record player is playing loud dance music.* SANDY, *a lively imp of about thirteen, stands near it, swaying to the music. She wears blue jeans. Several magazines are scattered on both beds and on the floor, along with a couple of cushions. An umbrella is lying on Sandy's bed,* L. GINNY, *a pretty girl in her teens, comes in* D L. *She wears a cute pair of pajamas and a robe.*]

GINNY [*annoyed, coming* C]. Sandy, I told you to leave my records alone! Look at the mess you've made of this room!

SANDY [*turning down volume of player*]. I was just reading—to pass the time.

GINNY [*looking around*]. Just reading! [*Picks up two cushions from floor.*]

SANDY [*moving* L C]. Till the pajama party.

GINNY. I had everything in order. [*Puts cushions on her bed,* R, *and picks up some magazines.*]

SANDY. I'm sorry, Ginny. [*Starts to straighten her bed,* L.] Do you think I ought to change into my new pajamas now?

GINNY [*turning*]. And why, may I ask?

SANDY. For the party, natch.

GINNY. Look, Sandy. I've told you. This is *my* party. For *my* club. No little sisters invited.

SANDY [*aggrieved, crossing* C]. Well, golly, this is *my* room, isn't it? Half of it, anyway.

GINNY. You're to sleep on the living room sofa tonight. Mother said so.

SANDY. Please, Ginny, let me stay. I've never been to a pajama party.

GINNY. No! I don't butt in when you invite your little friends.

SANDY [*indignantly*]. *Little* friends! [GINNY *ignores her and picks up more magazines, placing them in rack* U R.] All right! [*Pops down on her own bed.*] This is *my* bed, and you can't make me get out!

[MRS. REDMOND, *an attractive woman of about forty, comes in* D L. *She wears a coat and has her hat in her hand.*]

MRS. REDMOND. I'm leaving in a few minutes. Everything all right? [*Goes to mirror at dressing table to put on her hat.*]

GINNY. Mother, make Sandy get out of here. It's *my* party.

SANDY [*jeering*]. Have it in your own half of the room. [*Flops back on bed.*]

MRS. REDMOND. You might let her stay, Ginny. After all, she's not so very much younger than you are.

SANDY. I bet all they do at their silly old party is giggle and talk about boys!

GINNY [*coming down by her bed*]. We do not!

SANDY. Then why can't I stay?

MRS. REDMOND. The poor child won't have much fun, all by herself in the living room.

GINNY. She can read. [*Picks up a magazine and thrusts it at* SANDY.]

SANDY. I won't! [*Tosses magazine on floor.*]

MRS. REDMOND. Now, Sandy. Pick it up. [*Disgruntled,* SANDY *picks up magazine. To* GINNY.] I think you're being a little unreasonable.

GINNY. Mother, she acts too infantile. [*Crosses to her bed and sits.*]

SANDY. I suppose you're so grown up?

MRS. REDMOND. Girls, please! [*To* GINNY.] I've told you I won't interfere, since it *is* your party. But you might reconsider.

GINNY [*in a kinder tone, to* SANDY]. You can say "hello" to the girls, and stick around for a few minutes. But that's all.

SANDY [*sighing*]. Okay. [*Sits on her bed again.*]

MRS. REDMOND [*crossing* D L]. Well, that's that, I guess. [*Turns at door.*] Have a good time.

GINNY. We will.

SANDY [*gloomily*]. I won't. [MRS. REDMOND *goes out* D L. *Telephone rings.* GINNY *hurries* D L *to answer it, and* SANDY *crosses to record player.*]

GINNY [*into telephone*]. Hello. . . . Hi, Helen! You can come, can't you? . . .

[*There is a rap on the door* D L *and* NAN, *a vivacious teenager, comes in. She wears a coat over pajamas and a robe. She pauses at* L C.]

NAN. Your mother said you were in here. [*Opens her coat.*] I got a ride over, so I'm all ready.

GINNY [*to* NAN]. Good. [*Into telephone.*] Nan just came in. [*To* NAN.] Helen.

NAN. Anything wrong?

GINNY. Oh, no! [*Listens on telephone.*] Of course it's all right, Helen. What's your cousin's name? . . . I can loan her some pj's. . . . Tell her to walk right in when she gets here. . . . Okay. We'll see you a little later. 'Bye. [*Hangs up.*]

NAN. What's the matter with Helen?

GINNY [*crossing to* NAN]. She forgot about her music lesson tonight. She'll be here later. [*As* NAN *takes off her coat, displaying her pajamas and robe.*] Just darling!

SANDY [*starting record*]. I've got a dreamy pair, too. Wait till you see them.

GINNY [*warningly*]. You know what I said, Sandy.

SANDY [*frustrated*]. Oh, why was I born so young! [*Turns record player volume very loud.*]

GINNY. Shut that off! [SANDY *turns it low.*] We're going to have an extra girl tonight.

SANDY [*happily*]. Me?

GINNY. No, not you. [*To* NAN.] Helen's cousin Margaret is here for the week-end. I promised to loan her a pair of pj's. Hers are too lacy and Helen's don't fit.

NAN. The more the merrier.

GINNY. She's from Flemingdale. Helen says we'll like her.

SANDY. Everybody always likes everybody but me. [*Turns up volume again.*]

NAN [*at same time*]. Did you hear the police siren a few minutes ago?

GINNY. What?

NAN [*loudly*]. I said—[*As* GINNY *marches* D R *and shuts off record player.*]—did you hear the police siren a few minutes ago? [*Now she is shouting in the sudden quiet.* SANDY *giggles.* NAN *gives her a playful push toward* C *stage.*] Oh, you! [*Sits on bed* R. GINNY *sits beside her.*]

SANDY [*interested*]. What gives with the police? [*Sits on bench* U C.]

NAN. They're riding around looking for the Blue Light Burglar.

GINNY. In *this* neighborhood?

NAN [*nodding*]. Mother and I heard it on the car radio. Somebody reported seeing him—or her—just a little while ago.

GINNY. Him or *her?*

NAN. They say it could be a girl or a woman wearing slacks.

SANDY. Wow! I've been reading about the Blue Light Burglar in the paper every night. [*Dramatically.*] Sneaks into somebody's house—flashes a blue light—and says—"Your money or your life!"

NAN. It does give you a funny feeling, knowing somebody like that might be around.

SANDY [*eagerly*]. Maybe she'll come *here.*

GINNY. We don't have anything worth stealing.

SANDY. Is there a reward? Golly, I sure would like to capture a real live burglar.

GINNY. You watch too many TV shows.

SANDY [*defensively*]. *You* watch them, too.

GINNY. I don't believe them, the way you do. [*Warningly.*] And if you want to stay long enough to say "hello" to the girls, you'd better stop this talk about blue light burglars.

SANDY. Who's scared?

GINNY. You know what a fraidy-cat Carla is. She'd be scared half to death.

NAN. She's such a baby.

SANDY. *I'm* not afraid. [*Hopefully, rising.*] Maybe you'd like me to stick around—just in case?

GINNY. Definitely not! [SANDY *shrugs and sinks back on bench.*]

NAN. Aren't you even a little bit nervous, with your mother and dad out?

GINNY. Why should I be nervous? There really isn't anything here to steal. [*Gets up, going to telephone table.*] Except our club money. [*Indicates small box on table. Doorbell rings.*] I told the girls to walk right in. [*To* SANDY.] Maybe you'd better see if the door's unlocked.

SANDY [*rising*]. Okay. [*Goes out* D L. GINNY *moves* R C.]

NAN. We should have enough for play tickets now.

GINNY. Twenty-eight dollars.

NAN. Why, we're rich!

[CARLA *and* BECKY, *two more teen-agers, come in* D L. *Each carries a small overnight bag.* CARLA *is small and dainty, a real fraidy-cat.* BECKY *is a tall girl, athletic, with rather a loud voice. Both girls wear coats.*]

GINNY. Hi, girls!

CARLA [*coming* C *with* BECKY]. Hi!

BECKY. We brought our pj's.

GINNY. Put your coats in the guest room closet. [*Starts* U R.]

CARLA. Is everybody coming?

GINNY. Phyllis and Ellie, yes. Helen 'phoned she'd be a little late, but a cousin of hers is coming over.

CARLA. That's nice. You know what? The street light at your corner's out, and if Becky wasn't with me, I'd have been scared to death.

BECKY. What makes you think *I'm* so brave? [*Laughs and goes* U R.]

GINNY. Come on, Nan. Bring your coat. [NAN *rises, and she and* CARLA *follow* GINNY U R.]

[SANDY *comes in* D L *wearing perky pajamas. She poses with one hand on her hip and then walks around like a model at* C *stage.*]

BECKY. Not bad at all.

GINNY [*firmly*]. She's leaving us pretty soon. [*She,* CARLA, BECKY *and* NAN *go out* U R.]

SANDY [*annoyed*]. Oh, drat it! [*Looks after them, stamping her foot.*]

[*The door* D L *opens and* MICKY *comes in. She is a sweet and rather shy girl wearing slacks and a sport jacket. She carries a flashlight.* SANDY *turns as the door closes.*]

SANDY. Oh! Golly, you startled me!

MICKY. I'm sorry. Are you the only one here?

SANDY. Mother and Dad are out, and Ginny's with the other girls.

MICKY [*coming slowly toward* SANDY]. What's *your* name?

SANDY. Sandy. What's yours?

MICKY. Micky.

SANDY. Are you a friend of Ginny's?

MICKY. No, but——

SANDY. She's pretty busy tonight. She's having a party.

MICKY. A pajama party?

SANDY. Yes. How did you know?

MICKY. I've always wanted to come to a pajama party.

SANDY. Me, too, but I don't have any luck. [*Suddenly.*] Why are you carrying a flashlight?

MICKY. Because I cut through the alley and it's pretty dark. [*Hesitantly.*] Shall I sit down?

SANDY [*uncertainly*]. I guess so. [*Suddenly, with a whoop.*] Oh, now I know who you are! Golly, I've been dense.

[GINNY *and* NAN *come in* U R.]

SANDY. Ginny, this is Helen's cousin.

MICKY. Hello, Ginny. [GINNY *and* NAN *come* R C.]

SANDY. And Nan.

MICKY. Hello, Nan.

NAN. Hi!

SANDY. Her name's Micky, and look, she brought a flashlight because the alley's so dark.

GINNY [*smiling*]. I hope you didn't have any trouble finding your way.

MICKY. Oh, no!

SANDY. Ginny'll loan you a pair of pj's, Micky.

GINNY [*as name registers*]. Micky? I thought Helen said your name was Margaret.

MICKY [*hesitating slightly*]. Micky's just my nickname.

GINNY. Oh. Too bad Helen couldn't come with you.

MICKY. Yes, isn't it?

NAN [*suspiciously*]. Why couldn't she?

MICKY. She had some homework to do.

NAN. O-oh. [*Exchanges glances with* GINNY.]

SANDY [*importantly*]. Come with me, Micky. I'll take you to the guest room. [*To* GINNY.] Okay?

GINNY. Why, yes. [*Crosses past* MICKY *to* L C, *turning to look at her again.*]

MICKY [*as* SANDY *starts* U R]. It's very nice of you to have me here. [*Follows* SANDY U R.]

GINNY. You're very welcome. [SANDY *and* MICKY *go out* U R.]

NAN [*hurrying to* GINNY]. Ginny! Did you hear what she said?

GINNY. About homework? Yes, I heard.

NAN. But you told me Helen has a *music lesson.*

GINNY. That's right.

NAN. Then why does this girl say—homework?

GINNY. It's funny. [*Crosses* U R *and glances off.*]

NAN. And her name—she said it was Micky, till we said Margaret.

GINNY [*worried*]. I noticed that.

NAN [*crossing toward* GINNY, U R]. How do we even know for sure if she's Helen's cousin? Sandy called her that.

GINNY. And she agreed.

NAN. But don't you see—she could be *anybody.* Anybody at all, who wanted to walk into a house—and stay.

GINNY [*worried, crossing* C]. Yes, I—guess so.

NAN. Maybe she had some other excuse ready, but when we took her for Helen's cousin, she just went along with it.

GINNY. Oh, Nan—you don't suppose—but no!

NAN [*crossing down to* GINNY]. Why not? [*After a pause.*] She's wearing slacks.

GINNY. But we all do—now and then.

NAN. She carried a flashlight.

GINNY. That's not so very unusual. [*After a pause.*] Oh, we're being silly! [*After another pause, not so sure.*] Aren't we?

NAN [*ruefully*]. I guess so. She does seem like a nice girl.

GINNY. I'd feel better if I could get in touch with Helen.

NAN. Where does she take her music lesson?

GINNY. I don't know. [*There is a knock on door* D L.] Phyllis and Ellie, and I still haven't put out refreshments!

NAN. Go do it now. I'll let them in. [GINNY *hurries out* U R *and* NAN *opens door* D L.]

[PHYLLIS, *a cheerful plump girl, and* ELLIE, *a talkative miss, come in* D L. *They wear coats and carry small overnight bags.*]

NAN [*with a sweeping bow*]. Enter, my friends.

PHYLLIS. Are we the early birds?

NAN. Oh, no! You'd better hurry into your pj's.

ELLIE [*moving* C, *rattling on*]. Honestly, you know, I almost didn't come, because Johnny called me up for a movie date. But I think it's bad policy to be available at the last minute, don't you?

NAN [*who has paused* L C *with* PHYLLIS]. You'd miss our pajama party for an old movie?

PHYLLIS. *I* wouldn't. But I hope Ginny doesn't expect me to eat much because I'm on a diet.

NAN. Again? [*Starts* U R.]

PHYLLIS. What do you mean, *again?* I hardly eat enough to keep a bird alive.

NAN. Don't you know that birds eat *all the time?* [*Laughs teasingly.*]

ELLIE [*to* NAN]. Is that nice? We have to encourage Phyllis. [*To* PHYLLIS.] And I honestly do think you've lost maybe half a pound or so. [*Crosses* U R, *followed by* PHYLLIS.] You should have heard how mad Johnny was when I said I had another date! Maybe he'll call me earlier next time. He sure is cute. Don't you think so?

[MICKY *comes in* U R *wearing a pretty pair of pajamas.* NOTE: *To save time, they can be worn under her coat earlier.*]

NAN. Oh, sure, sure! Girls, I'd like you to meet Helen's cousin, Micky. Phyllis and Ellie. [*Greetings are exchanged.*] Be with you in a few minutes, Micky.

MICKY. Take your time. [NAN, PHYLLIS *and* ELLIE *go out* U R. MICKY *fusses with her hair at mirror. Then she walks around room looking at things. She goes to telephone table.*]

[GINNY *comes in* U R *carrying dishes of candy and potato chips.* MICKY *picks up the money box which is on top of the telephone book.* GINNY *pauses, startled.*]

GINNY. What are you doing?

MICKY [*turning*]. Getting your telephone book.

GINNY [*coming* C]. That's our club money.

MICKY. Is it? [*Sets box to one side and picks up telephone book.*] I thought I'd call Helen. [*Looks in book.*]

GINNY. Don't you know your own cousin's number? [*Puts dishes on record player table.*]

MICKY. I can never remember it.

GINNY. That's funny.

MICKY. Do you know the 'phone numbers of all *your* cousins?

GINNY [*a little embarrassed*]. No, I guess not. [*Quickly, crossing toward her.*] Let me call. I know her number.

[NAN *comes in* U R.]

GINNY. Micky wanted to call Helen, but I'll do it for her.

NAN [*crossing* C]. A very good idea.

GINNY [*to* MICKY *as she dials a number*]. You said she was doing homework?

MICKY. When I left, yes.

GINNY [*waiting*]. No answer yet.

NAN [*to* MICKY]. What kind of homework—geometry?

GINNY [*telephone to her ear*]. But Helen doesn't take——

NAN [*quickly*]. I was just wondering.

MICKY. I don't remember what it was.

GINNY [*hanging up*]. No answer.

NAN [*to* MICKY]. Helen told Ginny she had to take a music lesson.

MICKY [*crossing* L C]. That's right. Now I remember—it was some sort of music homework she had to do. About some composer.

NAN. O-oh. [*Exchanges glances with* GINNY.] So you remember now—after we told you.

MICKY. Yes, now I remember. [*Again girls exchange glances.* MICKY *stands* L C *and they stand on either side of her as they question her.*]

NAN. What high school do you go to, Micky?

MICKY. Regional.

GINNY. Where's that?

MICKY. In Ebbett's Crossing.

NAN. But I thought you lived in Flemingdale.

GINNY. Helen said you did.

MICKY. Flemingdale's the nearest city. Ebbett's Crossing is a sort of a suburb.

NAN. O-oh. [*Looks at* GINNY *again.*]

MICKY. Is anything the matter?

NAN. Oh, no! [*Tries to laugh.*]

GINNY [*trying to laugh*]. Everything's just fine. [MICKY *looks from one to the other, apparently puzzled.*]

[SANDY *comes in* U R *and turns on the record player.*]

SANDY. We're going to have a pajama parade. Everybody! [*As music starts.*] Here they come!

[SANDY *leads the parade, walking affectedly, as* CARLA, BECKY, PHYLLIS *and* ELLIE *come in* U R, *all wearing pajamas. As* SANDY *parades around the room with them following her,* NAN, MICKY *and* GINNY *join in.* PHYLLIS, *as she passes the candy dish, takes a piece. After they have paraded, they pose.* SANDY *claps.*]

SANDY. Yay for us! [GINNY *shuts off record player. Girls relax and find places to sit. Some take cushions from bed and sit on floor.* PHYLLIS *reaches again for candy before she settles.*]

ELLIE. I love pajama parties. They're so relaxing.

SANDY [*happily*]. I'll say! [*Takes a cushion and sits on floor, crossing her legs.*]

GINNY. Oh, no, you don't! [*Pulls* SANDY *to her feet.*]

SANDY. Aw, Ginny!

GINNY. I said you could stay till the girls come. Now—out! [*Points* U R.]

MICKY. Why don't you let her stay?

NAN. Because she's under age for this club, and rules are rules.

SANDY [*angrily*]. You don't have to be so mean about it. I *hate* your old pajama party! [*Stalks out* U R.]

CARLA. Poor kid—maybe she'll be nervous by herself.

GINNY. Not Sandy! [*Passes candy and potato chips around.*]

PHYLLIS [*reaching, then drawing back*]. No, I really shouldn't.

GINNY. Oh, go ahead!

PHYLLIS. Well, one won't hurt me. [*Takes one.*] Or maybe two. [*Takes another one.*]

NAN. How long have you been on this diet?

BECKY [*teasingly*]. It's called a nine-day diet, but she works at it one day each month.

CARLA. Oh, be nice!

BECKY. Well, here we are. What shall we do—sing?

MICKY. That would be fun.

GINNY. A few songs—then let's tell a Round Robin story. [*Puts dishes back on table and relaxes with others.*]

CARLA. Singing might make me feel better. [*Anxiously.*] I wasn't going to mention this—because you always call me a fraidy-cat—but did you know the police are looking for the Blue Light Burglar in this neighborhood?

GINNY [*ruefully*]. Yes, Nan and I knew. But we hoped you didn't.

CARLA. Oh, I'm not really afraid, with everybody here. [*After a pause.*] I guess I'm not.

PHYLLIS. But it makes a person sort of stop and think. [*Takes another piece of candy and settles down again.*]

GINNY. Nothing can happen to us while we're all together.

ELLIE. Maybe I should have gone to the movies with Johnny. If he stays mad at me, I'll just die.

CARLA [*plaintively*]. *I'll* die if that burglar comes prowling around here.

BECKY. Is the back door locked?

GINNY. I'm not sure.

BECKY. I'll go see. [*Gets up.*] And to make Carla feel safer, you'd better lock the front door, too. [*Goes out* U R.]

GINNY. Okay. [*Goes out* D L.]

PHYLLIS. Not that we're really afraid, but it's the sensible thing to do.

CARLA. Oh, my, yes! Although I can't help thinking of a

mystery movie I saw—they locked the doors after the burglar was already in the house!

MICKY. How awful!

CARLA. I couldn't sleep a wink all night after I saw that show. [*Shivers.*]

[BECKY *comes in* U R, *starting a popular song as she comes. She resumes her place as they all join in the song. Then* GINNY *comes in* D L *and sings with them as she settles down again.*]

GINNY [*when song is finished*]. Let's have another one. [*Starts a new song. This may be a lively one, and the girls clown a little, and laugh.*]

BECKY. Everybody feel better now? [*There are murmurs of "Much better!" "Sure!" "I'll say!"*]

GINNY. How about our Round Robin story?

PHYLLIS. I'm ready any time.

ELLIE. Who wants to start?

BECKY. I will. But maybe we'd better explain to Micky.

GINNY. It's fun. We all sit in a circle. One person starts a story—any kind of story——

CARLA. And the next one adds to it and leaves off in an exciting part——

NAN. And it goes all around the circle like that. [*Girls have pulled cushions to* C *and sit in a semi-circle on floor.*]

BECKY [*moving toward dressing table*]. Shall I turn out the lights now?

CARLA. No!

BECKY. But we always put the lights out. [*Turns off lamps on dressing table.*]

CARLA. Maybe you could leave just one light burning.

ELLIE. Honestly, Carla, you're getting worse all the time. What is there to be afraid of?

CARLA [*huffily*]. How do I know?

BECKY. The story's more fun in the dark. [*Turns off lamp beside high-backed chair. There are shivery cries.*] All set? [*Sits at one end of semi-circle. Next to her is* GINNY, *then*

NAN, PHYLLIS, ELLIE, CARLA, *with* MICKY *at the other end.*] I'm going to make it a real spooky one.

CARLA. Must you?

PHYLLIS. Oh, Carla, don't be such a baby! Let's all make it just as scary as we can.

BECKY. Here goes! [*In a foreboding tone.*] Once there was a very beautiful girl named Rochelle——

NAN. Why such a fancy name?

BECKY [*in her normal tone*]. Can I help it if that's what her parents named her? [*Goes on.*] Rochelle was a newspaper reporter, and one night——

NAN. Oh, not that again!

ELLIE. Hush!

BECKY. One night, when she was driving alone on a lonely country road—it was raining, and everything—suddenly her car stopped and she couldn't get it started again.

CARLA. Was she out of gas?

BECKY [*impatiently*]. How do I know? [*Continues story.*] Anyway, she noticed that there was a big, dark old house nearby, and all of a sudden she saw a light in the house, so she decided to go in and ask for help. The porch steps went creak—creak—creak as she climbed them, and when she went to knock on the enormous door, it opened of its own accord!

NAN. Nice going!

BECKY. Rochelle was afraid to go in, at first. But nerving herself, she entered the deserted living room of the old mansion. By the light of the moon she saw——

PHYLLIS. I thought you said it was raining.

BECKY [*quickly*]. The rain had stopped. Anyway, by the light of the moon she saw dust covers over all the furniture. Cobwebs brushed against her face——

NAN [*helpfully*]. And rats scurried away——

BECKY. Who's telling this? [*Continues story.*] Surely no one had been here for years! And yet, just a few minutes ago she had seen a light in one of the windows. And suddenly she noticed something else. The big grandfather's clock in the corner was ticking—ticking—ticking! [*After a pause.*] That's all for me. Go on, Ginny.

GINNY [*taking up story*]. Ticking—ticking—ticking! Rochelle knew somebody must have been here to wind that clock! Her own heart began to beat faster. Because, if somebody was here, why didn't they come to see what she wanted?

CARLA. Maybe they were hiding.

ELLIE. Quiet, Carla! It's not your turn.

GINNY. Rochelle took a deep breath and called out, "Is there anybody here?" No answer. The moon went under a cloud and it was very dark. Rain began to fall again. She heard strange banging noises. "It's only the shutters," she told herself. [*Suddenly girls hear faint banging noises. They all gasp.*]

CARLA. What was that?

PHYLLIS. There aren't any shutters on this house!

BECKY. Probably the wind.

CARLA. It wasn't windy when I came in.

BECKY. Well, it must be, now. Go on, Ginny.

GINNY. Rochelle was petrified with fear, but she tried to stay calm. Suddenly—she heard footsteps! [*After a pause.*] Nan, your turn.

NAN. The footsteps seemed to be coming up the cellar stairs. Rochelle rushed to the front door, determined to get out of this place—but the door was locked! And the footsteps kept coming! [*When she pauses, there is very faint sound of footsteps.*]

CARLA. *I* hear footsteps now!

ELLIE. I think I do, too!

CARLA. Maybe they're on the cellar stairs!

PHYLLIS [*alarmed*]. Ginny, is your cellar door locked?

GINNY. I—I don't know. I just never thought about it.

CARLA [*frantically*]. *Anybody* could get in!

ELLIE. Maybe somebody was here all the time!

BECKY. Oh, girls, act your age! We've told these stories before and nobody ever got scared.

CARLA. I always do.

BECKY. Oh, well—*you!* Go on, Nan.

NAN. Where was I?

GINNY. The footsteps.

NAN. Oh, yes! Now, I have to tell you that this old house was being used as the secret meeting place for a gang of counterfeiters.

BECKY. Must you be that corny?

NAN. No cornier than you were! [*Continues.*] The head of the gang was a wealthy society woman who made her own money.

BECKY. Nice work if you can get it!

NAN. She was determined to get rid of Rochelle before all was discovered. [*After a pause.*] Phyllis, you next.

PHYLLIS. Well, now, let's see. Rochelle was getting more and more frightened. Suddenly, she heard a moan. [*A faint moan is heard.*]

GINNY [*sharply*]. Who did that? Somebody's trying to be funny. Did you do it, Phyllis?

PHYLLIS. No. And I don't think it's one bit funny. [*Goes on.*] Well, she didn't know what the moan was, and neither do I. But in the meantime, this society woman crept closer—and closer—— Go on, Ellie.

ELLIE. Closer—and closer—and closer. And closer—and closer——

BECKY. Hey, how about a little action?

ELLIE. There wasn't any action yet. The room was very dark, and Rochelle couldn't see anything. But the woman just kept coming closer—and closer—— You go on, Carla.

CARLA [*shivering*]. Closer—and closer——

BECKY. How long does this go on?

GINNY. For goodness' sake, make something happen!

CARLA. Closer—and closer—and suddenly a voice cried out—— [*From behind high-backed chair* U R *a blue light is flashed on them and a voice calls out.*]

VOICE. Don't move, anybody, I've got you covered! [GIRLS *jump up, yelling. Blue light goes out and there are a few moments of confusion as they bump into each other in the dark.*]

CARLA. It's the Blue Light Burglar!

ELLIE. Help, somebody!

GINNY. Where did Micky go?

CARLA. Let's get out of here!

PHYLLIS. Who stepped on my foot?

NAN. Ginny, help me! I've got her!

GINNY. Where are you?

BECKY. Why doesn't somebody turn on the lights? [*At same time that these speeches are given very quickly, there is a steady pounding as if on front door, offstage* D L.]

NAN. Right here!

GINNY. Don't let her get away! [BECKY *turns on dressing table lights.* GINNY *and* NAN *hold* MICKY *at* L C. *She is struggling in a half-hearted way.* ELLIE, *by bed* L, *has umbrella raised as a weapon, and* PHYLLIS, U C, *is ready to swing dressing table bench.* CARLA *stands on bed* R.]

BECKY [*by dressing table, looking around*]. There's nobody here but us! [ELLIE *and* PHYLLIS *lower their weapons.*]

MICKY. Will you please let go of me?

NAN. You're the one!

GINNY. We thought so all along. [*Pounding is heard again, offstage* D L.]

BECKY. Somebody's at the front door. [*Goes out* D L.]

GINNY [*accusingly, to* MICKY]. You're not Helen's cousin, are you?

NAN. Admit you're not her cousin.

MICKY [*bewildered*]. All right, I admit it. But what difference does it make?

[BECKY *comes in* D L *with* HELEN, *a capable teen-ager. She carries a music roll and wears a coat, with pajamas rolled up under it.*]

HELEN. What's all the excitement? [*Stares at* MICKY.] Margaret—what's the matter? [*Crosses to her at* L C. BECKY *pauses* D L.]

MICKY [*near tears*]. They don't seem to think I'm *me.*

NAN [*surprised*]. Do you know her?

HELEN. Of course. My cousin Margaret. We call her Micky.

NAN. Your—cousin? [*Looks at* MICKY.] But you just said——

HELEN. Well, really, she's my aunt—Mother's youngest sister. But it saves a lot of explanations to call each other cousins. [*Takes off her coat.* GINNY *and* NAN *drop their hold on* MICKY'S *arms and step back, full of embarrassment.* CARLA *jumps down from bed.*]

GINNY. We thought she was the Blue Light Burglar. I—I'm awfully sorry, Micky.

NAN. I don't know what to say.

MICKY. Neither do I. [*Laughs shakily.*] But I guess it's all right now. [*As they talk, a figure in pajamas begins to crawl on hands and knees from behind high-backed chair toward door* U R. BECKY *sees her and signals to others for silence. She sneaks up on crawling figure just as it reaches door, and pulls a surprised* SANDY *to her feet. The surprise causes* SANDY *to drop flashlight she was carrying.*]

BECKY. *Here's* your Blue Light Burglar! [*Brings her* C, *as girls surround her.*]

GINNY. Oh, *Sandy!* [*Picks up flashlight.*] She covered Micky's flashlight with blue paper.

SANDY. You wouldn't let me come to your party.

[MRS. REDMOND *comes in* D L *with her coat and hat on.*]

MRS. REDMOND. Hello, everybody. [*Comes* L C.] Ginny, I just wanted to let you know I'm back. And by the way, I heard a bit of news on the car radio. The police have caught that Blue Light Burglar.

GINNY. They—have?

MRS. REDMOND. Yes. A man who had escaped from the State Pen. [*Briskly.*] Well, Sandy, I guess it's time for you and me to leave.

SANDY [*subdued*]. Yes, Mother. [*To* GINNY.] I really am sorry.

GINNY. I'm sorry, too. I guess I have acted rather infantile.

[*Puts an arm around* SANDY.] You can stay, if you still want to.

SANDY [*happily*]. Oh, boy! [MRS. REDMOND *smiles and goes out* D L.] Then let's go on with the story and I'll tell you what really happened in that deserted house! [*Grabs a cushion and sits near telephone,* D L. *All the other girls except* BECKY *sit down again in a semi-circle at* C, *and* SANDY *starts.*] All of a sudden, a voice cried out, "Who's there?" Rochelle ducked behind the door and waited. [BECKY *puts all lights out.*] There was a book-case behind her, and she picked up a big book, ready to de-fend herself to the death. As the wicked counterfeiter came near, Rochelle raised the book high—and brought it down with a crash! [*As she says this, she raises telephone book and brings it down hard, knocking money box and other articles from table. The crash makes girls scream again.* BECKY *turns on lights and they are in much the same posi-tions as before.* ELLIE, *by bed* L, *holds umbrella.* PHYLLIS *holds bench.* CARLA *stands on bed* R *and* HELEN *hunches on bed* L. GINNY, NAN *and* MICKY *huddle together at* L C. SANDY *holds telephone book high, looking down at damage she has done.*]

GINNY [*laughing in relief*]. Here we go again! [*They hold their poses as curtain falls.*]

CURTAIN